SHIB

By the same author:

Errata (1993)

To Bridget,

SHIBBOLETH

MICHAEL DONAGHY

All the best!

Michael Donaghy

Oxford   New York

OXFORD UNIVERSITY PRESS

Oxford University Press, Great Clarendon Street, Oxford OX2 6DP

Oxford New York

Athens Auckland Bangkok Bogota Bombay Buenos Aires
Calcutta Cape Town Dar es Salaam Delhi Florence Hong Kong Istanbul
Karachi Kuala Lumpur Madras Madrid Melbourne Mexico City
Nairobi Paris Singapore Taipei Tokyo Toronto Warsaw

and associated companies in
Berlin Ibadan

Oxford is a trade mark of Oxford University Press

First published as an
Oxford University Press paperback 1988
Reprinted 1989, 1990
Reprinted in Oxford Poets 1997

British Library Cataloguing in Publication Data

Donaghy, Michael
Shibboleth
I. Title
821'.914
ISBN 0-19-282564-X

Library of Congress Cataloging in Publication Data

Donaghy, Michael.
Shibboleth/ Michael Donaghy.
p. cm.—(Oxford poets)
I. Title. II. Series.
PS3554.O46535S5 1988
811'.54—dc19 88-9737
ISBN 0-19-282564-X (pbk.)

Printed in Hong Kong

*In memory of my parents
and in their honour*

Acknowledgements

Acknowledgement is gratefully made to the editors of the following periodicals, in which poems have appeared: *Poetry Review*, *Poetry (Chicago)*, *The Massachusetts Review*, *The Mississippi Review*, *The Chicago Review*, *Kansas Quarterly*, *Seneca Review*, *Orbis*.

'Machines' has appeared as a limited edition designed by Barbara Tetenbaum, published by Circle Press Publications, Guildford, Surrey. 'Smith' appeared as a limited edition, also designed by Barbara Tetenbaum, and published by Triangular Press, Madison, Wisconsin. 'Cadenza' was broadcast on Poetry Now (BBC, Radio 3). 'Shibboleth' was broadcast and appeared in pamphlet form as 2nd Prize Winner in the 1987 National Poetry Competition.

The quotation from Son House in 'Interviews' comes from Stefan Grossman's *Delta Blues Guitar*, Oak Publications, 1969.

This book replaces *Slivers* (Thompson Hill, Chicago 1985), and includes revised versions of some of the poems in that collection.

Thanks are due to Maddy Paxman, without whose help this book would have been completed in a fraction of the time.

MD

Contents

Machines

Dearest, note how these two are alike:
This harpsichord pavane by Purcell
And the racer's twelve-speed bike.

The machinery of grace is always simple.
This chrome trapezoid, one wheel connected
To another of concentric gears,
Which Ptolemy dreamt of and Schwinn perfected,
Is gone. The cyclist, not the cycle, steers.
And in the playing, Purcell's chords are played away.

So this talk, or touch if I were there,
Should work its effortless gadgetry of love,
Like Dante's heaven, and melt into the air.

If it doesn't, of course, I've fallen. So much is chance,
So much agility, desire, and feverish care,
As bicyclists and harpsichordists prove

Who only by moving can balance,
Only by balancing move.

Pentecost

The neighbours hammered on the walls all night,
Outraged by the noise we made in bed.
Still we kept it up until by first light
We'd said everything that could be said.

Undaunted, we began to mewl and roar
As if desire had stripped itself of words.
Remember when we made those sounds before?
When we built a tower heavenwards
They were our reward for blasphemy.
And then again, two thousand years ago,
We huddled in a room in Galilee
Speaking languages we didn't know,
While amethyst uraeuses of flame
Hissed above us. We recalled the tower
And the tongues. We knew this was the same,
But love had turned the curse into a power.

See? It's something that we've always known:
Though we command the language of desire,
The voice of ecstasy is not our own.
We long to lose ourselves amid the choir
Of the salmon twilight and the mackerel sky,
The very air we take into our lungs,
And the rhododendron's cry.

And when you lick the sweat along my thigh,
Dearest, we renew the gift of tongues.

A Miracle

This will never do. Get the bird
Of gold enamelling out of the den.
I'm *reading*. Gin, white as winter sun
Is blending juniper with oxygen.

Divinity is imminent. In the parlour
The crystal tinkling into words
Announces the arrival, through the mirror,
Of the host of stars and hummingbirds.

The angels have come early for the miracle.
They've gotten into the bar and drunk it dry.
Grinning, staggering, shedding feathers,
They can barely stand up, let alone fly.

One armoured, peacock feathered cherub
Holds my copy of the future to the glass
And reads backwards (as they do in heaven)
Of how this evening will come to pass.

The seraphim are fencing on the lawn.
Thrust and parry, tipsy physical chess.
'The Conversation of the Blades', they call it,
The actual clink and whirr, the holiness.

Analysand

(Judges 12: 5–6)

I've had an important dream. But that can wait.
I want to talk about Ephraim Herrero
And the cobalt-blue tattoo of Mexico
That graced his arm above the wrist.

We were his disciples back in school.
The hours I spent echoing his accent,
Facing off to the mirror, smoothing my jacket
Over the bulge of a kitchen knife. . .

Once he held a razor to my throat. . .
But we've been over that a hundred times.
Did I tell you he won the Latin prize?
So you see it was more than contempt and fear

That drew us to him. The day that he got done
For selling envelopes of snow in May
Behind Our Lady of Guadaloupe
We were as much relieved as lost.

When the day of judgement came we were in court
Backing the loser, the soul of perjury
Wearing a tie he must have stolen from me
And someone else's Sunday suit.

It was a kick to see him so afraid.
And when he took the stand and raised his hand,
And his sleeve went south of the Rio Grande
I saw at once which side I was on.

Which brings me to the dream, if we have time.
I'm wading across a freezing river at night
Dressed in that suit and tie. A searchlight
Catches me mid-stream. I try to speak.

But someone steps between me and the beam.
The stars come out as if for an eclipse.
Slowly he raises his finger to his lips.
I wake before he makes that tearing sound.

More Machines

The clock of love? A smallish, round affair
That fits in the palm. A handy prop
Like any of these: Compare
The pebble, the pearl, and the water drop.
They're all well made. But only one will prove
A fitting timepiece for our love.

To the pebble, the sun is a meteor,
The days a strobe, the years are swift.
Its machinery moves imperceptibly
Like the stars and continental drift.
But it's not for timing human love—it never *stops*.
Let us consider then the water drop

As it falls from the spigot during a summer storm
A distance of three feet. What does it see?
The lightning etched forever on the hot slate sky,
The birds fixed in an eternal V. . .
It falls so fast it knows no growth or changes.
A quick dog-fuck is all it measures

And it serves the beast as the stone serves God.
But our love doesn't hold with natural law.
Accept this small glass planet then, a shard
Grown smooth inside an oyster's craw.
Like us, it learns to opalesce
In darkness, in cold depths, in timelessness.

Deceit

The slate grey cloud comes up too fast.
The cornfield whispers like a fire.
The first drops strike and shake the stalks.
Desire attained is not desire.

The slate grey cloud comes up too fast.
However slyly we conspire,
The first drops strike and shake the stalks.
We cannot hold the thing entire.

The wind betrays its empty harvest.
The dead leaves spin and scratch the street,
Their longing for the forest
Forever incomplete.

Tell the driver to let you off
Around the corner. Be discreet.
Desire attained is not desire
But as the ashes of a fire.
The dead leaves spin and scratch the street.

The Present

For the present there is just one moon,
though every level pond gives back another.

But the bright disc shining in the black lagoon,
perceived by astrophysicist and lover,

is milliseconds old. And even that light's
seven minutes older than its source.

And the stars we think we see on moonless nights
are long extinguished. And, of course,

this very moment, as you read this line,
is literally gone before you know it.

Forget the here-and-now. We have no time
but this device of wantoness and wit.

Make me this present then: your hand in mine,
and we'll live out our lives in it.

Touch

We know she was clever because of her hands.
Hers, the first opposable thumb. Shards of her hip and skull
Suggest she was young, thirteen perhaps,
When the flash flood drowned her. Erect she stood
Lithe as a gymnast, four feet tall,

Our innocent progenitor.
Sleek furred technician of flint and straw.
Here are her knuckle bones.

I know her touch. Though she could easily snap
My wrist, she is gentle in my dream.
She probes my face, scans my arm,
She touches my hand to know me.
Her eyes are grey in the dream, and bright.

Little mother, forgive me.
I wake you for answers in the night
Like any infant. Tell me about touch.
What necessities designed your hands and mine?
Did you kill, carve, gesture to god or gods?
Did the caress shape your hand or your hand the caress?

'Smith'

What is this fear before the unctuous teller?
Why does it seem to take a forger's nerve
To make my signature come naturally?
Naturally? But every signature's
A trick we learn to do, consistently,
Like Queequeg's cross, or Whistler's butterfly.
Perhaps some childhood spectre grips my hand
Every time I'm asked to sign my name.

Maybe it's Sister Bridget Agatha
Who drilled her class in Christ and penmanship
And sneered 'affected' at my seven-year-old scrawl.
True, it was unreadably ornate
And only one of five that I'd developed,
But try as I might I couldn't recall
The signature that I'd been born with.

Later, in my teens, I brought a girl,
My first, to see the Rodin exhibition.
I must have ranted on before each bronze;
'Metal of blood and honey. . .' Pure Sir Kenneth Clark.
And those were indeed the feelings I wanted to have,
But I could tell that she was unimpressed.
She fetched our coats. I signed the visitor's book,
My name embarrassed back into mere words.

No, I'm sure it all began years later.
I was twenty, and the girl was even younger.
We chose the hottest August night on record
And a hotel with no air-conditioning.
We tried to look adult. She wore her heels
And leant against the cigarette machine as,
Arching an eyebrow, I added to the register
The name I'd practised into spontaneity—
Surely it wasn't—*Mr and Mrs Smith*?

It's all so long ago and lost to me,
And yet, how odd, I remember a moment so pure,
In every infinite detail indelible,
When I gripped her small shoulders in my hands,
Steadying her in her slippery ride,
And I looked up into her half-closed eyes. . .
Dear friend, whatever is most true in me
Lives now and forever in that instant,
The night I forged a hand, not mine, not anyone's,
And in that tiny furnace of a room,
Forged a thing unalterable as iron.

Cadenza

I've played it so often it's hardly me who plays.
We heard it that morning in Alexandria,
Or tried to, on that awful radio.
I was standing at the balustrade,
Watching the fish stalls opening on the quay,
The horizon already rippling in the heat.
She'd caught a snatch of Mozart, and was fishing
Through the static for the BBC
But getting bouzoukis, intimate Arabic,
All drowned beneath that soft roar, like the ocean's.
'Give it up,' I said, 'The tuner's broken.'
And then she crossed the room and kissed me. Later,
Lying in the curtained light, she whispered
She'd something to tell me. When all at once,
The tidal hiss we'd long since ceased to notice
Stopped. A flautist inhaled. And there it was,
The end of K285a,
Dubbed like a budget soundtrack on our big scene.
Next day I got the music out and learned it.

I heard it again in London a few months later,
The night she called me from the hospital.
'I've lost it,' she said, 'It happens. . .' and as she spoke
Those days in Egypt and other days returned,
Unsummoned, a tide of musics, cities, voices,
In which I drifted, helpless, disconsolate.
What did I mourn? It had no name, no sex,
'It might not even have been yours,' she said,
Or do I just imagine that she said that?

The next thing I recall, I'm in the dark
Outside St Michael's Church on Highgate Hill.
Coloured lights are strung across the portico,
Christmas lights. It's snowing on me,

And this very same cadenza—or near enough—
Rasps through a tubercular PA.
How did I get here?

Consider that radio, drifting through frequencies,
Suddenly articulate with Mozart.
Consider the soloist playing that cadenza,
Borne to the coda by his own hands.

Letter

It's stopped this morning, nine hours deep
And blank in the sun glare.
Soon the loud ploughs will drive through the drifts,
Spraying it fine as white smoke,
And give the roads back. Then I'll sleep
Knowing I've seen the blizzard through.

First your papers must be put in order.
In drawer after drawer your signatures wait
To wound me. I'll let them. There's nothing else in your hand.
No diaries, no labelled photographs, no lists.
But here's a letter you sent one year
With my name scratched carefully on onionskin.
Empty. Man of few words, you phoned to explain.
It's the only letter you ever wrote me.
And you mailed the envelope.

No relics here of how you felt;
Maybe writing frightened you, the way it fixed a whim.
Maybe ink and graphite made
Too rough a map of your fine love.
But remember one August night
When I was weak with fever and you held my head
And reeled off 'The Charge Of The Light Brigade'
(Of all things) to calm me. You had it by heart;
By breath. I'd hear that breath when you talked to yourself
If not to me, or muttered in your sleep,
Or read aloud, like monks and rabbis do,
Breath that would hardly steam a mirror,
Whispering like gaslight. Day after year
After night I missed the words.

I always will. At the funeral I recall
A man with God's book open whispering.
'The letter kills,' said Paul,
'The spirit giveth life.' But my mouth was shut
When I spoke the word goodbye.

Three weeks have passed. Three weeks the clouds clenched
Low in the sky, too cold to snow until last night

When I rose to the slap of sleet on the glass and hard wind
And saw my face lamplit in the dark window,
Startled that I looked older, more like you.
Then half asleep, half frozen, close up against the pane, I mouthed
Father. Frost fronds quickly swirled and vanished
As if you read them back to me. Your breath
Making the blizzard silent,
The silence quiet, at last,
The quiet ours.

Slivers

Somewhere fore of the heaped ropes and sonar housing
Cunning men hunch windward who know by bone
By sextant or the lodestone or the planets, to plot,
To give the bearings. Alone of night fares
They know the latitudes of home.

And there are sea towns where even children
Have that art because they grip
The present from the cunning and the hunched.
They grip it, and they serve it, and they drown.
But I am miles from any craft or ship.

Across the wide lot glint glass slivers
From the splintered windshields of stripped cars.
In this place without water, in this hour past awe,
I grip these gifts which only look like stars
And draw vague lines across uncrafted seas,
And map by these.

Shibboleth

One didn't know the name of Tarzan's monkey.
Another couldn't strip the cellophane
From a GI's pack of cigarettes.
By such minutiae were the infiltrators detected.

By the second week of battle
We'd become obsessed with trivia.
At a sentry point, at midnight, in the rain,
An ignorance of baseball could be lethal.

The morning of the first snowfall, I was shaving,
Staring into a mirror nailed to a tree,
Intoning the Christian names of the Andrews Sisters.
'Maxine, Laverne, Patty.'

Quorum

In today's *Guardian*, the word *quorum*
is spelled the same as *oqürum*,
the only surviving word of Khazar,
according to the *Great Soviet Encyclopaedia*.
Oqürum, meaning 'I have read'.

The original pronunciation is lost forever,
but I weigh three syllables in my palm
against 'paprika' and 'samovar',
'cedarwood' and, for some reason,
'mistletoe'. I have read. . .

an entire literature,
and enacted all that it describes.
On a winter morning, in an ochre room
that we can never enter, the resonance
of those imaginary consonants

the elders whisper over ancient documents
flickers the blood bright shadow
from a glass of tea.

Auto da Fé

Last night I met my uncle in the rain
And he told me he'd been dead for fifty years.
My parents told me he'd been shot in Spain
Serving with the Irish volunteers.
But in this dream we huddled round a brazier
And passed the night in heated argument.
'El sueño de razón. . .' and on it went.
And as he spoke he rolled a cigarette
And picked a straw and held it to an ember.
The shape his hand made sheltering the flame
Was itself a kind of understanding.
But it would never help me to explain
Why my uncle went to fight for Spain,
For Christ, for the Caudillo, for the King.

Ramon Fernandez?

I met him when I fought in the brigade,
In Barcelona, when the people had it.

Red flags snapped above the tower clock
Of what had been renamed the 'Lenin Barracks'.
The ancient face was permanently fixed,
If memory serves, at half eleven.
Dead right twice a day.

Fernandez played guitar each day at noon
In the plaza beneath the barracks tower,
Hawking his revolutionary broadsides.
And as he sang he stared up at the clock
As if he half expected it to move.

I recall the way he played the crowd
Sure as he played his lacquered blue guitar.
I recall the troop trains pulling from the station,
White knuckles over carbines, boys' voices
Singing the anthems of Ramon Fernandez.

And I wonder if anyone caught on but me.
The songs the fascists sang across the wire
Were his, the same he sang, got us to sing.
A few words changed, not many. *Libertad*,
Hermana Libre, I have them all by heart.

One day he vanished back across the front
And later, when the town was under siege,
A stray round hit the barracks clock and cracked
Both iron hands clean off but left the face
To glare like a phase of the moon above the burning city.

Partisans

Imagine them labouring selflessly,
Gathering evidence through the long winter.
Now they bring their case before you.
'Let us arrive at the truth together'

They say, these patient women and men.
The seconds tick by in the small cell.
The fluorescent bulb whines like a dentist's drill.
They want you to spell the names again.

Majority

Foreign policy does not exist for us.
We don't know where the new countries are.
We don't care. We want the streets safe
So we vote for the chair. An eye for an eye.

Our long boats will come in the spring
And we will take many heads.
The name of our tribe means 'human being'.
We will make your children pray to our god in public.

News Item

The trampled corpses
Stacked in the lobby
Are all that remain of the literal-minded.

Among the missing
Are the little girl who shouted 'Fire'
And those of us who remained seated
Savouring the sheer
Theatre.

Pornography

The bodies of giants shine before us like a crowded fire.
One might quite credibly shout 'Theatre'.
I can't watch this. Instead, I'll stare at the projector beam
The smoke and dust revolve in and reveal.

Remember my story?
How one grey dawn in Maine I watched from my car
As a goshawk dove straight down toward the pines?
I said the dive was there before the hawk was,
Real as a wind shear before the blown snow reveals it.
The hawk became its aim, made one smooth purchase
In a splintering of twigs. A hare squealed, and I watched the bird
Slam the air in vain till it gave up and dropped its catch.
I told you how I sat and watched the rabbit die,
And described blood steaming on the frosted gravel.

Remember how angry you were
When I told you I'd made it up?
That I'd never been to Maine or owned a car?
But I told my tale well, bought your pity for the hare,
Terror for the hawk, and I served my point,
Whatever it was.

And remember that time
I was trapped in a cave and saw shadows on the limestone wall?
When the scouts freed me and carried me to the cave mouth
The true light burned my eyes like acid. Hours passed
Before I found myself safe in the Maine woods, resting in my car.

THE END is near. The final frame of 'Triumph Of The Will'
Slips past the lens and the blank flash blinds us.

Footage from the Interior

I

Boyoko is teaching me to wait.
We squat behind wrist thick
Stalks of palm and listen
For the faint drumming of engines.

Just after sundown
The trawler slides around the headland.
The motor coughs, whinnies, and stops.
We watch and wait

As one by one the running lights
Go out across the dark lagoon.
Voices carry from the deck across the still water.
Not the words, but the sweep and glide of words.

Theirs is a tongue of tones and cadences
And Boyoko knows from the rhythm alone
Whether to slip away unseen
Or wait for rifles.

II

Boyoko is teaching me Lekele.
'Our word for *lagoon*
Can also mean *poison*, or *promise*,
Depending on the syllable stressed.'

A blue moth thrums
The windscreen of the idling jeep,
Slamming its tiny head against the glass
In urgent Morse.

Boyoko beats the word *freedom*
On the steering wheel.
'Try it.' I try it.
'No,' he tells me, 'You said *bacon*.'

III

Boyoko's been teaching me the 'talking drums'.
Side by side, we stand among the chickens
In the yard behind his hut.
I'm roasting. And my fingers ache.

Today when his son walked past
Boyoko lost me, slapping rhythm
Over rhythm. I stopped, he smiled,
And we resumed our lesson.

Minutes passed,
And then the boy came back
Bringing two cans of cold brown beer.

Khalypso

The development of complex cell communities in the zygote thus resembles the creation of heavier and heavier elements in the star's contraction. . . .

R. Profitendieu, *Birth*

Cast off old love like substance from a flame;
Cast off that ballast from your memory.
But leave me and you leave behind your name.

When snows have made ideas of the rain,
When canvas bloats and ships grow on the sea,
Cast off old love like substance from a flame.

Your eyes are green with oceans and you strain
To crown and claim your sovereignty,
You leave me and you leave behind your name

And all the mysteries these isles retain.
But if the god of sailors hacks you free,
Cast off old love like substance from a flame

Until you're in a woman's bed again
And make her moan as you make me,
'Leave me and you leave behind your name.'

The brails go taut. The halyard jerks, the pain
Of breeching to the squall and all to be
Cast off, old love, like substance from a flame.
Now leave me. I will live behind your name.

A Disaster

We were ships in the night.
We thought her rockets were fireworks.

Our radio was out, and we didn't know
The band was only playing to calm the passengers.

Christ, she was lovely all lit up,
Like a little diamond necklace!

Try to understand. Out here in the dark
We thought we were missing the time of our lives.

We could almost smell her perfume.
And she went down in sight of us.

Starlet

Berenice affects her April dialect.
Buds bloom stiffly to her rapid vowels, mud breaks
For apple-green shoots. Nude, descending
A staircase, she trails a shady wake of geometries
Like a ship stirring shoals of luminous algae.
Freely she warms to the folk whose soles
Thump brownly on her marble floors.
She breathes their garlic air wheezed
From hot concertinas and, in the cool evening,
She unbinds her starry skein of hair,
The heavens bespangling with dishevelled light,
Gives interviews.

Interviews

Yvette lets a drop
Of red blot brilliant
On the white,
Fresh bedsheet.

1913. She looks up
From painting her toenails.
Marcel is ahead of his time,
Yvette is still dressing.

He finds a note
From Apollinaire:
'Knight to
Queen's rook three,'

And checks the board.
He looks at the little horse, snaps
It across the room,
A distance

> *Of fifty years*
> *To a studio in Neuilly*
> *Cassette wheels spinning*
> *Throughout the interview*
> *And he thinks of bicycles.*

Q: *Where does your anti-retinal attitude come from?*
A: *From too great an importance given to the retina.*

1913. It's getting late.
The sun obscures
As it illuminates
Garden and gardener
Whose hedge-clippers snip. . .

'Zip me,'
Yvette says over her shoulder,
Stepping into her yellow pumps,

The ones with the goldfish in the heels.

> *Wait, I'll flip*
> *The cassette to erase*
> *'Interview with Delta bluesman*
> *Son House 1/5/68'*

Q: *What about Willie, was he very good at making up verses?*
A: *Yeh, he could make up verses pretty good. Yeh, 'cause he'd start on one thing*
he'd let near about every word be pertaining to what he pronounced what he was
going to play about. That's the difference in him and Charley and me, too.
Charley, he could start singing of the shoe there and wind up singing about that
banana.

Marcel looks at the little horse
And wonders whether
'Nude Descending a Staircase'
Is the name of his entry
In the armory show

Or if 'Nude Descending a Staircase'
Is his entry
In the armory show.

Within three years
His friends will drop in the trench
Screaming, chlorine searing
Their throats and noses raw.
Apollinaire in the field-hospital,
Red on white gauze,
Will imagine the random trajectories
Of fragments, shrapnel, chessmen.

A: *Since Courbet, it's been believed that painting is addressed to the retina. Before, painting had other functions: it could be . . . moral.*

Stop.

I'd be playin' by myself sometime, nobody will be around me whatever to hear it, and my mind will be settin' on some crazy things — Scripture or jes names of songs, any old thing. 'Fore I know anything tears'll be coming down and I put that guitar away.

Back from the Salon,
Yvette removes
Her yellow shoes.
The gramophone
Clears its throat
For Satie.

Yvette, Yvette,
So much to drink.

From tonight on you'll be Rrose,
Rrose Selavy.

Later he'll undress her.
Setting long glove

And stocking down at right
Angles. Here comes

The bride.

> *Duchamp then produced*
> *A miniature machine for me*
> *To photograph: watch parts*
> *Clicking and skidding*
> *Across clear, flat glass*
> *Toward two, gnat sized yellow shoes.*

But now they laugh in the dark.
Lighting her cigarette,

Marcel makes a world around them,
A short, shining world.

Remembering Steps to Dances
Learned Last Night

Massive my heart, the heart of a hero, I knew it,
Though I was ten, pimpled, squint eyed, dung spattered.
I strung a bow, and memorized a brief heroic song
(I'll sing it for you later), left my goats in my father's yard,
And then went down to the ship.
Many men massed at the dock, loud their laughter.
But the king listened, noted my name, gave me wine,
A little patriotic speech, and sent me home
To the goats and the tedium and the ruminant years.
Once I made a song about the king and his distant plundering
And the hoard of memories, wondrous, he was gathering.
It's a shame you didn't bring your guitar.

Then one summer, when I was older,
And the king was long since missing in action,
Men came from Achaia to court the lonely queen.
The nights got loud with drums and laughter echoing from the
        palace,
Women's laughter, and the smell of roasted lamb.
What would you have done? I pounded on the gates one morning,
Rattled my arrows and stamped and sang about my hero-heart.
They seemed to understand . . . Or didn't mind my lying,
And they opened the gates on another world.
Beauty. Deception. Of weaving, of magic, and of the edge of the
        known world
When the light fails, and you fall dead drunk across the table,
All these we learned in our feasts and games amid the grey eyed
        women.
Clever men and many we waited, the queen to choose among.

I know you came to hear me sing about the night the king came
     home,
When hero slaughtered hero in the rushlit hall,
Blood speckling the white clay walls wine dark.
I can't. I'd stepped outside when the music stopped mid-tune.
Alone in the dark grove, I heard no sound but distant insects,
And the sound of water, mine, against the palace wall.
And then I heard their screams, the men and women I'd spent that
     summer with.

What would you have done?
I staggered home in the dawn rain, still half drunk,
Forgetting one by one the names of my dead friends,
Remembering steps to dances learned that night, that very night,
Back to my goats, goat stink, goat cheese, the governing of goats.

The Tuning

If anyone asks you how I died, say this:
The angel of death came in the form of a moth
And landed on the lute I was repairing.
I closed up shop
And left the village on the quietest night of summer,
The summer of my thirtieth year,
And went with her up through the thorn forest.

Tell them I heard yarrow stalks snapping beneath my feet
And heard a dog bark far off, far off.
That's all I saw or heard,
Apart from the angel at ankle level leading me,
Until we got above the treeline and I turned
To look for the last time on the lights of home.

That's when she started singing.
It's written that the voice of the god of Israel
Was the voice of many waters.
But this was the sound of trees growing,
The noise of a pond thrown into a stone.

When I turned from the lights below to watch her sing,
I found the angel changed from moth to woman,
Singing inhuman intervals through her human throat,
The notes at impossible angles justified.

If you understand, friend, explain to them
So they pray for me. How could I go back?
How could I bear to hear the heart's old triads—
Clatter of hooves, the closed gate clanging,
A match scratched toward a pipe—
How could I bear to hear my children cry?

I found a rock that had the kind of heft
We weigh the world against
And brought it down fast against my forehead
Again, again, until blood drenched my chest
And I was safe and real forever.

Rational Construction

Along a girder, high above the pavement
A man is carrying a man-length mirror.
Crowds gather to track his movements,
His one foot easing over the other.
We squint, and the sun snaps down from the glass
Finding faces. But up there they keep
Their eyes on their feet. We bask in their flash,
But they owe us no 'intuitive leap'.

The Dreamer and the Dreamed Have Dinner

Rien n'est, en effet, plus désenchantant, plus pénible, que de regarder, après des années, ses phrases. Elles se sont en quelque sorte décantées et déposées au fond du livre; et, la plupart du temps les volumes ne sont pas ainsi que les vins qui s'améliorent en vieillissant; une fois dépouillés par l'âge, les chapitres s'éventent, et leur bouquet s'étiole.

Huysmans

It is the ripest hour. He stands before the window,
Scans the night and sighs, clouding the pane.
Road. Streetlamps. Shops. The solstice light
Smooths a pool of similes disguised as names.
His carafe, half drained, opaque in the dark,
Conceals before it is uncorked and poured.
Beyond mere sense, so does his heart
Until the clock, clicks locked in random clusters,
Resolves arhythmically. Chuck: a car door?
'Her Citroën,' he thinks, because he trusts her
Cycles and her secret female arts.
All wines retain impurities. A sip
Numbs an unexamined intention as she knocks.
His welcomes are readied with overkill workmanship.

'Late again.' They talk. They spend the twilight
On his terrace rereading *Against the Grain*.
'Like tears in different colours. . .' (She *abhors*
It when he does this. Large drops of warm rain
Dapple their shoulders, so they drift indoors.)
She stretches and yawns; he persists unaware. . .
'Like gazing at a photographic detail
Of a wineglass, unable to say what it is.'
Why must he slow the sunset with these flares?

'Oh for a beaker full of the warm south,'
She offers. Stumped, he laughs for sheer decorum.
Nothing slowly happens. Their shadows stretch out
In a half-light charged with visionary boredom:
Pale whims, faint furies, dim endeavours
Await the age's end, the commonsense of darkness.
When will darkness come? When will the lovers?

Reader,

I shuffled through a hemlock thicket
Breaking bracken underfoot.
The snapped twig snared me. I went down

Pitching among wet cakes of leaf
And brushed against soft bark,
Sloughed the dark husk off. There,

In the wet air, in the cold,
The inviolable purity of new wood
Stiffened the night against itself.

I coupled with it. There was light
Like foxfire and on the road the wind twisting
Voices through the powerlines.

Now kneel before the painted brambles,
In front of the fan, with the lights off
And try to read this page. Just try.

Seven Poems from the Welsh

Sion ap Brydydd (d. 1360) was a contemporary of the undisputed master of classical Welsh poetry, Dafydd ap Gwilym, and it is in the shadow of Dafydd's achievement that Sion's significance has been so unfortunately obscured. A commoner by birth, Sion borrowed a sum from the court of Owain for his education to the career of court poet. He held that post for less than a year when he was dismissed for neglecting to repay the loan and he spent his remaining years among the criminal element of Aberystwyth. Perhaps as a result, his diction is a mixture of poetic 'mandarin' Welsh and earthy demotic. And this, together with his obsessive use of difficult forms, has marked him as an eccentric in the history of Welsh poetry. For example, recent computer analysis of *Y Hiraeth*, his 30,000-word description of the interior of a heron's egg, has revealed two columns of slant rhyme weaving through the text line by line in a perfect double helix pattern. How such a poem could have been written under such exacting formal constraints is a puzzle. Why it was written is a positive enigma.

He is best known, however, for his 30-syllable *englynion*. These short poems were not *composed* in the sense in which that term applies to the writing of English poetry. Rather, they were thought to have *obtained*, like Japanese *tanka* and *haiku*, as the complete and inevitable response to a split second of painfully acute perception. To the objection that the preconceived form of the poem shapes that perception, Sion would answer that during such moments neither poet, poem, nor subject, can be distinguished one from the other. In this mysterious way, he believed, all his englynion were faint echoes of a single unwritten poem which, if pronounced, would so perfectly unite the souls of author and listener that they would inhabit each other's bodies and exchange destinies. This poem, he believed, drifted just beyond his grasp 'like a snowflake of complex geometry which dissolves when it lights on the tongue'.

In the winter of 1360 Sion was beheaded for the crime of adultery. Here are my translations of seven in a sequence of twenty-nine englynion he wrote in the tower of Pentraeth on the eve of his execution.

*

I

Morfydd, daughter of Gwyn,
The dells are bright with snow.
Driven with cruel purity,
They'll take you for one of their own.

II

Cloves and cedar smoke in the air,
Swarms of dragonflies in the long grass.
I unlaced her muslin gown.
No help from her.

III

Smooth the skin on a bowl of milk
And on the warm hollow of her thigh.
The soft turf is slow to warm,
And after this, shallow breathing.

IV

The moment you touch the whorl of my ear
With the tip of your tongue
Is a gold dome over itself.
So is the moment after.

XXVII

Dull the journey.
Feeble and muttering the old men.
Amber and sweet the wine of spring.
I won't have autumn's vinegar.

XXVIII

Dull the journey.
Long the road reeled in toward the lantern.
Patience is cold soup
And salt in the sugar bowl.

XXIX

Say this rhyme, reader, aloud to yourself.
Gladly I'd bear your senility and incontinence,
Let you warm this bed of hay,
Rattle these chains, write these lines.

The Natural and Social Sciences

We come to Straidkilly to watch the tide go out.
A man is loading a wicker basket
With small, complicated pink crabs.
'Have we missed it?' we ask, 'the tide?'
And he, with sincere assurance,
'It'll be back.'

A girl inspects an upside-down bike
On the road to Tubbercurry.
I stop to help but she rights it on its wheels,
Shoves off, ticking in the light rain.

Musicians in the kitchen, Sunday morning in Gweedore.
An American with a tape recorder and a yellow notebook.
'What was the name of that last one?'
The piper shrugs and points to the dark corner.
'Ask my father.'
The American writes 'Ask My Father.'

The Last Tea of Rikyu

Early evening and a summer presence.
A moist wind moves on the roofs of Horyu-Ji,
Flicks iridescent beetle wings beneath wrought copper;
It is the daily rainstorm.

But we are in the tea hut in Rikyu's garden.
Rikyu, slandered without grace or respect,
Condemned by a dull and intolerant patron,
Is granted an hour of life.

The whirr of insects,
The master's hands, the lanterns,
And the damp hiss of the kettle
Show forth from the moment.

We take our places.
    'Do not be sad.
    We will meet every time there is tea.'
The unsteady cup warms my hands.

The others withdraw like shadows.
I remain to witness the gesture.
Rikyu unwraps bands of black silk
From the short sword.

His eyes are clear.
    'Have we not already died
    Who live beyond fear and desire?'
I weep for humility and gratitude

And do not see the shock, the body buckling.
This is how it always begins;
A jolt, the world whirls within us,
A raindrop hesitates, then hits the roof.

The Noh

After 1868 when the Shogunate was overthrown and the Noh fell
out of favour, the costumers and mask makers who had previously
produced so many rich effects became careless in their pro-
ductions, offering only a few crude variations.

Yamashiro, *A History of Noh*

From the bright glass greenhouse steamed with palms
She brings you from sleep to where she has tacked
A mask of wood to a trellis arm
To seduce you. She *is* abstract.

Thunderstorms tonight, she warns.
No stars suspend above the palms
But gro-lights crackle on the leathery leaves.
Tonight, in her arms,

Conquer the noble opacity of the mask
Back to its maker who planed the cheapest wood
Against the grain and pilfered the design
Arse deep in debt and carving against a deadline.

His early masks were perfect. So were mine.
But roles come and go, standards and wood decay
And split. One can no longer say,
'Had we but world enough and time',

You just make do. Unclench your fists.
This delicate cheek and skin of painted pine
Provide your mind for silence by themselves.
He taught no truth to shape who chiselled this.

The gong tolls classically. It is twelve,
And the drops against the glass become a hiss.
Kiss her. Her rhythmic breathing levels
Beyond her name and beauty to a 'yes'.
Together leave the greenhouse its emptiness.

Inheritance

My father would have cherished an heir,
but he remained unmarried.

Science was his mistress, and after science,
my mother. But we were provided

with a collection of seashells
second only to the emperor's.

I regret I will not live
to see the final specimen auctioned.

It is the jewel in the diadem.
A sulphur nautilus,

wound like the spring of a gold watch.
My mother would not part with it in life.

When he died I saw his name
in the *Journal of Marine Genetics*. Sharp,

peach-coloured spikes of coral
are named for him.

The Origin of Geometry

High above Thebes the huge birds glide
Describing smaller and smaller circles.
Below, the Greek boy tells his teacher

That all things, the cinnamon air at dusk
And the red sand, are the 3D
Writing of the gods.

Just so, he says, his alphabet's a world
Dug in red sand with a cypress stick.
He stands above it like a god.

But the old man carves pictures
On a lump of clay. Moon. Scarab.
'See? See?' Young Thales points

To the first letter of his name.
'Round like the moon.' The old man squints
Brushing a fly from his face.

In just a moment
They will lose the gods forever.
But now the cranes fly round and round

Into the maelstrom of the lengthening light.

The Penitent

At times also I have been put to confusion and driven to despair of ever explaining something for which I could not account, but which my senses told me to be true.

Galileo Galilei, *Two New Sciences*

Unseen, dogs cough on the colourless beach
Over waves, incessant, incessant. If all this sand
Were dried and ground and polished to a lens
That order now fanned out too far
For us to see could focus through it.
But see, they subside, Procyon and the Twins.
Defaced by day, their imagined musculature
Crushes and sharpens a tiny brilliance on my sin,
Igniting kindling. My eyes are stung with smoke;
Too much truth in too grey a place
And too combustible a heart. These days
I move in quiet circles and take for nourishment
Light's white gristle, the unprismed lie.
God shines. The tide looks solid in his love,
And yet it *does* move.

The Don't Fall Inn

The blue pool illuminated, the cocktail lounge is open.
Rippling with liquid glints like firelight,
The lit bellhop gazes in terror
At the diving board and the cool, deep mirror.

Here is the Register of Revelations.
Use my pen. 'Edvard . . . and . . . Mimi . . . Munch.'
We hear muffled voices through the walls.
A strangely submarine effect. Like bubbles.

Something is terribly wrong
And the porters come to dust it.
They are hoovering as we leave at dawn.
Although the word 'TV' is out,
They flash the sign against the hail grey sky:
REASONABLE RATES   OLYMPIC SIZE POOL
                    . . . IN EVERY ROOM

Goodbye.

Riddle

I am the book you'll never read
But carry
Forever,

One blunt page, garlanded
By daughter
Or lover.

You already know two-thirds by heart.
And I'm passing weighty for a work so short.

Envoi

Go away. All that's over.
No more fluttering, squirming, crawling, running.
I've achieved stillness, clarity.
Since the tide gave up this one rock
And I'm the only point to reckon by
Many of you have taken me for a sign.
Stop. Stay on the deep.
Wing back down the round sleep of waters.
Deceive them, tell them it never ends.
Give me peace.

But the speech of skulls is strange to birds.
Weary, eager for crumbs and Noah's praise,
The dove snapped half the glittering twig
Curling green in the eye socket,
Clutched it, flew.

OXFORD POETS

Fleur Adcock
Moniza Alvi
Kamau Brathwaite
Joseph Brodsky
Basil Bunting
Tessa Rose Chester
Daniela Crăsnaru
Michael Donaghy
Keith Douglas
D. J. Enright
Roy Fisher
Ida Affleck Graves
Ivor Gurney
David Harsent
Gwen Harwood
Anthony Hecht
Zbigniew Herbert
Tobias Hill
Thomas Kinsella
Brad Leithauser
Derek Mahon
Jamie McKendrick

Sean O'Brien
Alice Oswald
Peter Porter
Craig Raine
Zsuzsa Rakovszky
Christopher Reid
Stephen Romer
Eva Salzman
Carole Satyamurti
Peter Scupham
Jo Shapcott
Penelope Shuttle
Goran Simić
Anne Stevenson
George Szirtes
Grete Tartler
Edward Thomas
Charles Tomlinson
Marina Tsvetaeva
Chris Wallace Crabbe
Hugo Williams